SUPER SILLY SCHOOL JOKES AND RIDDLES

NEIL YAMAMOTO

D0892726

TOR ®

A TOM DOHERTY ASSOCIATES BOOK
NEW YORK

SUPER SILLY SCHOOL JOKES AND RIDDLES

Copyright © 1991 by RGA Publishing Group, Inc.

A Tor Book
Published by Tom Doherty Associates, Inc.
49 West 24 Street
New York, NY 10010

ISBN: 0-812-59375-8

First edition: February 1991

Printed in the United States of America

0 9 8 7 6 5 4 3 2 1

What is the difference between a locomotive engineer and a teacher?
    One minds the train, the other trains the mind.

What do you call a pickle that can add, subtract, divide, and multiply?
    A cuculator.

What kind of table has no legs?
    The multiplication table.

How can you tell the difference between a school bus and a grape?
    Jump on top of it for awhile; if you don't get any juice, it's a school bus.

What kind of teacher teaches you how to play the flute?
A private tooter.

What happens to principals after they retire?
They lose most of their faculties.

What do astronauts get when they do all their homework?
    Gold stars.

Name six wild animals.
    5 tigers and a lion.

What is the most important subject a witch learns in school?
Spelling.

Why aren't hens allowed in school?
   Because "fowl" language isn't allowed.

8

Teacher: *What pines have the longest and sharpest needles?*

Allen: Porcupines.

How do they serve smart hamburgers?
    On honor rolls.

What's the difference between a train and a teacher?
    One says, "Choo-choo!" and the other says, "Don't chew!"

Teacher: *Why do bells ring at Christmas?*

Pete: Because someone pulls the rope.

Principal: *What should a teacher know before trying to instruct a student?*

Teacher: More than the student!

When is a student in trouble for something he didn't do?
    When he didn't do his homework.

Why shouldn't you mention the number 288 in front of the teacher?
    Because it's too gross. (two gross = 288)

Teacher: *What did they wear at the Boston Tea Party?*
Meg: T-shirts.

11

Teacher: *Where do we get condensed milk?*
Sam: From short cows.

Why are fish so smart?
    Because they live in schools.

What is the first thing a gorilla learns in school?
    The Ape-B-C's.

Teacher: *What do you call an animal that eats raw meat?*

Linda: A bad cook.

Teacher: *Where was the Declaration of Independence signed?*

Terry: At the bottom.

Teacher: *If you received ten dollars from ten people, what would you have?*

John: A new bike!

Teacher: *Please finish this phrase: "Cleanliness is next to..."*

Aaron: Impossible!

What is the world's smartest insect?
  The spelling bee.

Teacher: *Carol, do you know who the 20th*
          president of the United States was?
Carol: No, we never met.

Teacher: *Please give me three reasons why the earth is round.*

Johnny: Because my mother says so, my father says so, and you say so.

Teacher: *Are you chewing gum?*
Student: No ma'am. I'm Ronnie Jones.

Teacher: *Why was George Washington buried at Mount Vernon?*
Bobby: Because he was dead.

Teacher: *Who was the fastest runner of all time?*
Sue: Adam, he was first in the human race.

Teacher: *Bennie, what did they do at the Boston Tea Party?*

Bennie: I don't know, ma'am. I wasn't invited.

Teacher: *Who was Joan of Arc?*

Jamie: Noah's wife.

Why was the geometry teacher boring?
   Because he was a square and he talked in circles.

Why shouldn't you put grease on your hair the night before a test?
   Because, if you did, everything might slip your mind.

Do teachers ever need to wear glasses?
   Only if their pupils are bad.

Teacher: *Why does the Statue of Liberty*
stand in New York Harbor?

Max: Because it can't sit down.

Teacher: *Where do fish sleep?*
Dan: In water beds.

Teacher: *What do we have in December that isn't in any other month?*
Joe: The letter "D".

Teacher: *How did Columbus' men sleep on their ships?*
Mark: With their eyes shut.

Teacher: *Jeff, if you cut an apple in two, what would you have?*

Jeff: Two pieces.

Teacher: *Correct. Now, if you cut a pear in four, what would you have?*

Jeff: Four pieces.

Teacher: *Very good. If I cut a banana in eight, what would I have?*

Jeff: Eight pieces.

Teacher: *Good. Now, if I added it all up, what would I get?*

Jeff: Fruit salad.

Teacher: *Stevie, your report on pets is the same as your brother's.*

Stevie: Of course, it's the same pet!

Teacher: *What did Benjamin Franklin say when he discovered electricity in lightning?*

Erik: Nothing. He was too shocked to speak.

Dad: If I had seven oranges in one hand and
      eight oranges in the other, what would
      I have?

Son: Big hands!

If I had 2 hamburgers and you had 2
hamburgers, what would we have?
      Lunch.

!?!LUNCH!?!

Teacher: *What are the Great Plains?*
Phil: Boeing 747s.

Teacher: *Where is the ocean deepest?*
Alma: At the bottom.

Teacher: *How can you tell the difference between an adult snake and a baby snake?*

Cindy: The baby has a rattle.

What happened when the teacher wrote, "Please wash" on the chalkboard?
    The school janitor took a bath.

What did the mother firefly ask the teacher?
   "Is Junior bright?"

What is green, wet, and teaches school?
   The teacher from the Black Lagoon.

What happens to teachers when they retire?
   They lose their class.

Teacher: *Jane, how do you spell "banana"?*
Jane: B-A-N-A-N-A-N-A-N-A-N-A…
         well, it's in there somewhere!

Who belongs to the Ghoulies PTA?
    Mummies and deadies.

Where's the best place to find a book about trees?
    A branch library.

What's the difference between a dressmaker and the school nurse?
    One cuts the dresses and the other dresses the cuts.

What's the smartest food in the market?
    Grade "A" eggs.

Why do soccer players do well in school?
Because they use their heads.

*What kind of code did the Viking learn
in school?*
Norse code.

How did the student get a flat nose?
    His teacher told him to keep it to the grindstone.

Why is the school yard larger at recess?
    Because there are more feet in it.

Five girls walked to school under one umbrella. How many got wet?
None. It wasn't raining.

Teacher: *What birds are found in Portugal?*
Myron: Portu-geese.

How do science teachers count atoms?
    They atom (add 'em) up.

*If you throw a teacher in the water, what does
he become?*
    Wet.

Teacher: *How can you tell the difference between a girl moose and a boy moose?*

Penny: By his moose-tache.

Teacher: *How did Thomas Edison's invention of the light bulb help society?*

Ken: If it weren't for him, I'd have to watch TV by candlelight.

How does a textbook about zombies begin?
  With a dead-ication.

Teacher: *Can you tell us where elephants*
  are found?
Joe: We don't have to find elephants.
  They're so big, they don't get lost.

Why wouldn't the student study history?
    Because she thought it would be better
    to let bygones be bygones.

Where do math teachers go to eat?
    The lunch counter.

What is the difference between a teacher and a doughnut?
> You can't dunk a teacher in a glass
> of milk.

Typing Teacher: *Well, Connie, are you typing any faster?*

Connie: Yes, I am. I'm up to thirteen mistakes a minute.

Jeff: *Did the teacher like your report on sheep ranchers?*
Lisa: No.
Jeff: *What did he say?*
Lisa: It was baaaaaaaaaaad.

Why did Robin Hood steal from the rich?
Because the poor didn't have any money.

WELCOME
TO
SHERWOOD
FOREST
(ESPECIALLY
YOU RICH
FOLKS!)

Why did the student eat nickels for lunch?
   Because the teacher wanted to see some change in him.

What was the best student at agricultural school voted by his classmates?
   The kid most likely to sack seed.

Is writing a report on an empty stomach harmful?
No, but writing on paper is better.

What kind of person likes to study oceans?
Someone who likes to study things in depth.

Mabel: *Mom, I got 98 today!*
Mom: That's great. What did you get it in?
Mabel: *A 50 in English and a forty-eight in math.*

Teacher: *Name an animal that lives in Africa.*
Shelly: A lion.
Teacher: *Very good. Now name another.*
Shelly: Another lion.

What kind of school teaches you to make ice cream?

Sundae school.

Teacher: *Donnie, you only got six mistakes on your spelling test this week.*

Donnie: Really? I'm doing better.

Teacher: *Yes, you are. Too bad there were only eight words on the test.*

Teacher: *If there were ten cats in a boat and one jumped out, how many would be left?*

Sara: None, because they were all copycats.

Teacher: *Do you know where we get*
          brown eggs?
Lisa: Dirty chickens?

Is learning about the desert fun?
    No, it's too dry a subject.

Margaret: *Why did George Washington stand up in the boat while crossing the Delaware?*

Anne: Because he didn't want to row.

Why don't more people go to coffee-maker's school?

Because most folks can't take the grind.

*Why did the two-headed monster do well
in school?*
    Because two heads are better than one.

Dad: *How are you doing in school,
          Johnny?*
Johnny: Oh, I'm doing the same as George
          Washington.
Dad: *What do you mean?*
Johnny: I'm going down in history.

What three days have no school?
    Saturdays, Sundays and holidays.

What's green and teaches music?
    Johann Sebastian Broccoli.

What kind of coach has no wheels?
    A football coach.

What did Paul Revere say when he got on his horse?
   "Giddy-up!"

*What kind of test does a vampire take
in school?*
    A blood test.

Ms. Trent: *Who can tell me who invented
            fractions?*
May: Henry the Eighth.

Do Hawaiian children enjoy school?
   No, they are too "lei-ed" back.

Why did the duck like to tell jokes in class?
   Because he was a quack-up.

What is the world's longest punctuation mark?
   The hundred-yard dash.

Principal: *I'm happy to see you enjoying school. What's your favorite subject?*

Tim: Recess.

How do most students like school?
    Closed.

How is a judge like an English teacher?
They both hand out long sentences.

Where do female ghosts attend class?
At an all-ghouls school.

Teacher: *Where did our Founding Fathers stand when they landed at Plymouth Rock?*

Maria: On their feet!

Why do spiders spin webs?
    Because they never learned how to knit.

Where can you find prehistoric cows?
   In a moo-seum.

Why does it take so long for an elephant to get ready for school?
   Because he has to pack his trunk.

Sally: *If April showers bring May flowers, what do May flowers bring?*
Allie: Pilgrims.

Teacher: *To what family does the rhinoceros belong?*

Penny: I don't know, Mr. White. No one in our neighborhood has one.

Can a Science book walk?
   Only if it has enough footnotes.

Teacher: *What do you do when you're lost in the woods?*

Scotty: Call for my mommy.

How do you begin a school report about palm trees?

Once a-palm a time...

Joanie: *When do you wake up in the morning?*

Joey: Oh, about halfway into my English class.

In math, when do two and two make more than four?

When they make twenty-two.

Teacher: *Barry, use the word "avenue" in a sentence.*

Student: I avenue bicycle.

When are classrooms able to see?

When they have pupils in them.

Teacher: *What kind of keys can't open any door?*

Al: Piano keys.

How many books can you put in an empty school bag?

One. After that the bag is no longer empty.

What do growling animals receive on their report cards?
     Grrrrrrrrades.

Mr. Jones: *What causes trees to become petrified?*

Jamie: The wind; it makes them rock.

What do you get when you cross a chicken with a teacher?
 Eggsams.

Mr. Darwin: *Shelley, what is an atom?*
Shelley: Eve's friend.

Teacher: *Gloria, can you tell me what a vacuum is?*
Gloria: Well, I think it's another word for brain. Daddy says I have one in my head.

Teacher: *Sally, what side of the pie is the left side?*

Sally: The side that isn't eaten.

Why was the cannibal expelled from school?
     For buttering up the teacher.

How do you begin a class report about a chess game?
     Once a pawn a time...